Tom,
I'm glad that you and
Jim shared so many stories!
Jan

Tales of Uncle Tompa

Tales of
Uncle Tompa
The Legendary Rascal of Tibet

Compiled and Translated by
Rinjing Dorje

Illustrations by Addison Smith
Foreword by Wendy Doniger
Introduction by Marilyn Stablein

STATION HILL ARTS
BARRYTOWN, LTD.

Published under the Station Hill Arts imprint of Barrytown, Ltd., Barrytown, New York 12507, as a project of The Institute for Publishing Arts, Inc., a not-for-profit, federally tax exempt, educational organization.
Web: www.stationhill.org
E-mail: Publishers@stationhill.org

Grateful acknowledgement is due to the National Endowment for the Arts, a Federal Agency in Washington, DC, and by the New York State Council on the Arts for partial financial support of the publishing program of The Institute for Publishing Arts, Inc.

Distributed by Consortium Book Sales & Distribution, Inc. 1045 Westgate Drive, Saint Paul, MN 55114-1065.

Cover design by Susan Quasha.
Text typesetting and design by Susan Quasha.
Illustrations (including cover) by Addison Smith.

Library of Congress Cataloging-in-Publication Data
Rinjing Dorje, 1949-
    Tales of Uncle Tompa : the legendary rascal of Tibet / Dorje
Rinjing ; illustrated by Addison Smith.
      p. cm.
    ISBN 1-886449-40-6 (pbk. : alk. Paper)
    1. Uncle Tompa (Legendary character) 2. Tales—China—Tibet.
GR377.R56 1997
398.2'09515'02—dc21   97-12947
                                         CIP

Printed in the United States of America.

Contents

TALES of UNCLE TOMPA

OTHER TALES

I would like to dedicate this book to the memory of my late parents, and to my children, Guru and Dewa.

I am deeply indebted to my friend Tom Strickland for his support and encouragement.

Author's Note

Storytelling is a important aspect of traditional Tibetan culture. Even in recent times there were professional storytellers and bards called Lama Mani who traveled from village to village to tell stories and recite epics. But also many elderly persons were storytellers in the villages. There are stories of various regions, gods and demons, animals and people. There are epics, myths, and fables with fantastic twists and plots. This orally transmitted tradition was perpetuated as the elderly passed it on to the new generation. But ever since the invasion of Tibet by the People's Republic of China, and the subsequent diaspora of the Tibetan people to far-flung places across the globe, the old oral traditions could slowly fade away. While some collections of Tibetan tales have recently appeared in both the West and in China, many story cycles remain uncollected.

Among all these stories, my favorites are of the renowned trickster, Agu Tompa. 'Agu' means 'uncle' in Tibetan, and so I have called him Uncle Tompa throughout this book. You will not find a Tibetan who does not grin luminously when you simply mention the name Agu Tompa.

Many people believe this rogue actually lived in southern and central Tibet around the thirteenth century. But there is simply no proof of this. I have compiled and translated these stories from my childhood memory using plain language about sexual matters, as Tibetans always do when joking in their own tongue. I hope you will not find this offensive.

Living in America for the last twenty years, I have seen many books written about Tibet, but I have yet to see one on Tibetan humor, one of the most enduring and endearing characteristics of the Tibetan people. I hope in reading my book you will find both laughter and relaxation from the frenzy of everyday life.

I would like to thank my friends Ter Ellingson and Larry Epstein for their help in correcting and editing my manuscript, Marilyn Stablein whose warm friendship for nearly three decades has guided me through the literary world, and Professor Wendy Doniger of the University of Chicago for her thoughtful Foreword. My sincere gratitude to David Hoffman of Dorje Ling Publishing who initially published this book some twenty years ago, and to all the folks at Station Hill Press who have given this work a second lease on life.

Rinjing Dorje
Seattle, Washington
1997, Year of the Fire Ox

Foreword

I have treasured my copy of the first edition of Rinjing Dorje's *Tales of Uncle Tompa* ever since Stephen Beyer gave me a copy in Berkeley back in the late 1970s. Beyer himself had written a fine book about a different aspect of Tibetan culture (the cult of Tara), and his appreciation of the stories made a deep impression on me. I was sorry when both Beyer and the book left the academic world, Beyer to become a lawyer, *Tales of Uncle Tompa* to go out of print. Now one, at least, has returned, and is most welcome.

What charms me most about these stories is the way in which they flicker back and forth between the uniquely Tibetan and the universal. Anyone familiar with the folklore, indeed the literature, of other parts of the world will recognize certain themes, particularly "trickster" themes. The scene in which Uncle Tompa says he is named "Vagina," anticipating the moment when his victim will want to call for help and will be misinterpreted and hence ignored ("Vagina is hurting me") reminded me of the scene in Homer's *Odyssey* in which Odysseus says he is named "Nobody," anticipating, in the same way, the moment when Cyclops would call for help and be misinterpreted and hence ignored ("Nobody is attacking me"). The scene in which Tompa fabricates not merely the costume of a transvestite but the physical body of a transsexual reminded me of the similar trick played by the North American trickster whose stories were documented by Paul Radin (and interpreted by C.G. Jung in his introduction to Radin's book). And the scene in which Uncle Tompa takes back his urine recalled the fountain-pen techniques reclaiming not urine but semen, perfected by Indian yogis (who called it "Vajroli"), and documented by Mircea Eliade.

How are we to explain these convergences? The yogic technique, with its Indian provenance, is almost certainly historically connected with Tibet and can be explained by borrowing. The transsexual story might also be explained by borrowing or diffusion, since it participates in a shared body of myth (which includes tricksters, shamans, earth-diver myths and much else) that connects East Asia with North America across the ancient land link of the Bering Straits. The Odyssean parallel might, just perhaps, be an Indo-European survival, coming to Tibet through India. But I rather suspect that we are dealing here with some very basic human themes that cannot be entirely explained by historical contacts, even though they may have been enhanced by such contacts. And what makes this particular telling, Rinjing Dorje's telling, unique is not just the Tibetan details but his own unique voice. These are hilariously dirty stories, unabashedly sexual and politically incorrect indeed. (I doubt that many feminist readers will be amused by the total disregard for the feelings of the women whom Tompa rapes). They have a brutal innocence which transcends any culture, including ours. They travel well, like good wines. I am delighted to see them back in print again.

Wendy Doniger
Mircea Eliade Distinguished Service Professor of the History of Religions,
The Divinity School, University of Chicago

Introduction

From the nomadic yak herders whose tales first enraptured Rinjing Dorje as a young boy tending the family's grazing livestock on the high mountain slopes of northern Nepal, to the nuns and monks in the monastic enclaves of remote Himalayan valleys, the mere mention of Uncle Tompa's name brings laughter and smiles of recognition. Tibetans cherish this wily character who easily pokes fun at the rich, the miserly, and the gullible.

Tibet is a land of austerity. Frigid winters make travel as well as communication between towns and villages extremely difficult. Short summers limit food harvests. When Rinjing Dorje was growing up there was limited contact with the West and few forms of entertainment: no radios, televisions or movie palaces; no bowling alleys, shopping malls or sports arenas. In the remote mountainous regions itinerant storytellers called Lama Mani traveled from monastery to village telling stories in exchange for a few coins or a handful of the roasted barley flour called *tsampa*. Outside the monastery doors or in front of a dome-shaped stupa these storytellers regaled old and young with moral tales that explicated aspects of Buddhist Dharma. The twelve realms of existence, for example, from birth to adolescence, marriage, childbirth and death were the subjects of popular stories. Uncle Tompa's ribald tales add a humorous folkloric dimension to a richly entertaining storytelling tradition.

Mystery shrouds Uncle Tompa's heritage. Some claim he was a monk who lived during the thirteenth century. Others claim he was a reincarnation of the Buddha of Compassion, called Chenrézig in Tibetan (or Avalokiteshvara in Sanskrit), whose multiple arms and eyes constantly reach out in the ten directions to save those in need. Uncle Tompa's foolishness echoes the "crazy wisdom" of such "mad" yogis as Drukpa Künlek, a popular spiritual adept of the 16th century who went about as a vagabond. The latter composed—often in an intoxicated and debauched state—songs and Dharma verses of great mastery to instruct the people he met on his travels. However, unlike the stories of Drukpa Künlek who is revered as a saint, there are no overt Dharma teachings in Uncle Tompa's tales. Rather, he is the ostensible schlemiel whose carefully plotted foolishness results in pleasurable rewards like food, drink or the stolen or beguiled charms of a woman. To win the heart and pocketbook of one naive but rich man, for instance, Uncle Tompa disguises himself as a woman, ties a sheep's lung over his penis to simulate a vagina, then lures the man into marriage!

Because Uncle Tompa in his ingenuous and slapstick way champions the common folk, the tales reinforce peasant values which encourage independence and bravery while mocking artifice, pretense and strict authoritarian rule. In this way Uncle Tompa—"Uncle" translates "*Aku*," the Tibetan avuncular term of endearment that reflects how close he is to the hearts of those who know, tell and hear his stories—still serves as a traditional folk hero for Tibetans today. His stories are well-known throughout the diverse and now disparate Tibetan community.

In one Scheherazadesque twist, Uncle Tompa entices a senior lama of a monastery into letting him share the lama's meal of the delicious steamed dumplings called *momos*. One by one he eats them with obvious pleasure, stretching out the dramatic revelation as the greedy lama hangs on his every word (seeming to promise riches), thereby also spinning an amazing tall tale for our ears. On another occasion he outwits a king by eating the best *tsampa* which he was supposed to be guarding.

Whether a cup of *chang*, barley beer, or a lavish feast for the whole village, Uncle Tompa reaps the fruits of his cleverness. In a tradition consistent with the Jataka Tales where the Buddha lived previous lives as tigress, monkey or snake, it's not far-fetched to find Chenrézig's wisdom emanating through a rascal like Uncle Tompa. His chicanery is a guise. Uncle Tompa accomplishes the impossible; he transmutes submission into mastery, absence into abundance and foolishness into wisdom.

Uncle Tompa's adventures feature trickery and hyperbole not so different from those of the Native American Coyote or the Middle Eastern Mullah Nasruddhin or any number of other tricksters of greater or lesser renown. Yet with the exception of the tale of a lama's curse that creates a fantastical crop of penises—which Uncle Tompa promptly turns to profit by setting up shop in front of a nunnery, even catching the eye of the head Abbess herself!—most of his adventures remain, unlike, say, Coyote, well within the realities of daily life.

Many of his tricks revolve around language, especially its distortion and misuse. Before slipping into the king's daughter's bedchamber Uncle Tompa takes the clever precaution of misnaming himself Vagina; later, cries of "Vagina is bothering the princess" of course bring no response. Even when caught and threatened with execution he manages to outwit the king with a claim—that the daughter is pregnant. Since no king would want a widow for a daughter, Uncle Tompa is not only pardoned but allowed to marry the princess he seduced.

Uncle Tompa may act like a simpleton but he is more literate than some kings. As a boy Uncle Tompa was sent to a monastery to learn to read, write and recite the scriptures. In one tale he is hired to read the holy scriptures to a family. When on another occasion he tosses a frozen pile of excrement, dusted with lime, onto the king's lap, the dubious missile carries a so-called miraculous inscription which Uncle Tompa reads aloud to the illiterate king. "This is Shit from Heaven. He is the luckiest King when it drops in his lap." Immediately the pious king touches the excrement to his forehead in a gesture of respect, then nibbles a piece before placing the rest on his altar. Uncle Tompa's scatological effrontery here is an act of revenge for an earlier punishment meted out by the king. This is Uncle Tompa the indefatigable Everyman, standing up against social injustice; his bold gesture lays bare, more poignantly than political argument, the social and economic disparity between the classes.

At a time when Tibetan culture in the country of its origins is being systematically annihilated, what makes Rinjing Dorje's collection so valuable is that he has preserved a vital part of his cultural heartland. The adventures of a beloved folk hero/prankster have moved from oral to written (hi)story and the pleasurable enrichment of present and future readers. These stories, the first Uncle Tompa tales to be transcribed and translated into English, contribute not only to the records of an endangered oral Tibetan literature, but also to ethnography and the study of oral tradition generally, especially the trickster cycles. In so diligently collecting these tales and so remarkably rendering them in English, Rinjing Dorje translates something more than stories—the cherished storyteller's role itself, from live performer to vivid and memorable prose, worth reading again and again. In so doing he shares something as dear to his own heart as it is true to his native wit, the irresistible and compelling Tibetan sense of humor and *joie de vivre*.

Marilyn Stablein

Uncle Tompa
As a Young Monk

I n the olden days in Tibet, there were no schools for the children of poor families where they could go and learn to read and write. On the other hand, rich and noble families hired private tutors to teach their children.

The only way for the children of ordinary folks to become literate was to send their boys to the monasteries and their girls to the nunneries. There, if one were accepted, he or she would be ordained as a novice. Then one would be assigned as a pupil or protégé of a senior monk who became responsible for the pupil's welfare and education while in the monastery.

Some of the monasteries had several hundred to several thousand monks. Many of the senior monks had anywhere from five to ten youngsters living under their care, and they were taught everything from reading and writing to monastic ceremonial chants.

When Uncle Tompa was a young boy, his parents decided to send him off to a monastery to study. After some months of living in the monastery, young Uncle Tompa asked his master if he could go to visit his parents. The master granted his request.

Since his parents were so poor, young Uncle Tompa quickly returned to the monastery. As he walked into his master's room, he smelled something good and saw that his master was enjoying a big plateful of the most delicious Momo or steamed meat dumplings. His long journey had made him hungry and tired.

He wished to share his master's sumptuous meal, but in Tibet it is absolutely impolite to ask to share someone else's food.

He hastily went up to his master and asked, "Master! Master! Do you know what happened on the trip to my parents?"

Enjoying his meal, the master asked with little interest, "What?"

"On the way to my parents, I found a bag full of gold," the young novice gleefully announced.

Suddenly interested, the master looked up in surprise and gave young Uncle Tompa a dumpling, asking him with huge smile, "What happened to the gold?"

Contentedly munching the Momo, Uncle Tompa said, "I told my parents that I'm going to take the gold to my master." The greedy master gave him two more Momos and pressed on, "Then what happened, tell me!"

The young novice said, "My parents said that they should have half and I should take half to my master!"

The master gave him three more dumplings and asked, "What did you say to them then?"

"I argued with them, saying I intended to take the entire bag to my master, because he's provided me with everything I need."

The master, filled with greed, gave him the rest of the Momos and asked, "Then what happened?"

By now, the master's plate was all empty. Young Uncle Tompa stretched his arms in the air and yawned, slowly rubbed his eyes and said, "While I was arguing about the gold with my parents, I suddenly woke up."

Uncle Tompa
Sleeps with the King's Daughter

ncle Uncle Tompa was traveling in a far away part of Tibet when he arrived at a small kingdom. There he found the king had a very pretty virgin daughter. Because of her beauty, many people wished to marry her. Uncle Tompa was no exception. He too wished to become her husband, or at least to have the chance to sleep with her.

One day Uncle Tompa donned very ragged clothes and stood by the gate of the king's palace. He waited for several days when finally the king came out riding a horse. Uncle stood up, bowed and asked if he could have a job in the palace.

"What can you do?" the king asked Uncle.

"Your Lordship, I can be your sweeper in the palace bedrooms. I'm very good at that." The king gave him the job.

Uncle worked there for several days. One morning he walked into the king's bedroom with his broom to sweep. The king asked him, "Boy, what's your name? I forgot to ask you."

"Your Lordship, I cannot tell you my name because it's disgraceful and I'm too bashful to tell you!"

"You must tell me your name; otherwise, how can I call you?"

Uncle said, "My parents, very unfortunately, gave me the name 'Penis,' Your Lordship!" So the king started calling the boy 'Penis.'

The next day, Uncle went to sweep the queen's bedroom. She too asked Uncle his name.

"I don't want to tell you because it is a very bad name and I'm too embarrassed to tell you, Your Ladyship!"

She insisted he tell her, so Uncle finally admitted, "My name is 'Vagina'!" So the queen started calling him 'Vagina.'

Later he went to the daughter's bedroom, where she too asked him his name. Because Uncle had noticed she ate peas a lot, he replied, "My name is 'Peas'!"

Then one night Uncle hid under the daughter's bed. As soon as she went to bed, Uncle climbed out from underneath, grabbed her, and started raping her. She was very frightened and started shouting, "Mommy! Daddy! 'Peas' is bothering me! 'Peas' is bothering me!"

Her mother yelled at her, "I told you not to eat so many peas! Now they're bothering you at night! Well, we can't do anything except call a physician."

Again, the daughter shouted loudly, "Ah! 'Peas' is bothering me!" Her mother came to see what was the matter with her daughter.

She saw 'Vagina' screwing her, and she cried out, "Ah! 'Vagina' is bothering our daughter, 'Vagina' is bothering our daughter! Come and see!"

Hearing all this commotion, the king shouted at them "Are you both going berserk? What do you mean, 'Vagina' is bothering her?" So, finally, the king went to see for himself what was going on. He arrived just in time to see 'Penis' jump off his daughter and spring out the window.

The king shouted and hit the gong to summon his guards. Soon the guards came and bowed down. He ordered them, "'Penis!' 'Penis!' Go out and catch that 'Penis'!" They all ran out into the courtyard and stood there holding their own penises.

When the king came out and saw what the stupid guards were doing, he could not believe his own eyes. He got very angry and yelled, "I told you to hold the man whose name is 'Penis'!"

Finally they figured out what the king wanted. The guards rushed out and started chasing Uncle. After some time, they caught him and brought him to the king's court.

The king ordered his men to execute 'Penis' in public for the crime of raping his daughter. When all the subjects had gathered, and he was just about to be executed, Uncle shouted out, "Well! Your Lordship! I'm speaking my last words to you. Listen to me! I'm ready to die; I don't care about my death. But I've slept with your daughter anyway. I'm quite sure your daughter will become pregnant. I don't know if the child will be a son or a daughter. Anyway, your daughter won't be called 'princess' from now on. She'll be called 'widow' if she doesn't have a live husband."

The king thought that there was some merit to what 'Penis' had said, so he ordered, "Wait! Don't execute him now!" The king thought very carefully and then decided to pardon him. Shortly afterwards, Uncle became the king's son-in-law.

Uncle Tompa
Sells Penises at the Nunnery

nce upon a time, a couple was sowing their field. They had hired a few fieldhands to help them. It was lunch time. All the hands were taking their lunch, including the couple who owned the field. Tibetans enjoy laughing and making fun of each other. So, while everyone was busy laughing, having fun, and telling dirty jokes, a very holy Lama walked by. The Lama greeted the couple with the customary Tibetan expression, "What are you doing?"

The couple started to say that they were sowing seeds for their crop, but since they were right in the middle of telling dirty jokes, the answer that slipped out was, "Well, we're sowing penises in our field."

Everybody laughed because of the slip, but the Lama was embarrassed by their reply. So he cursed them, "MAY EVERY SEED OF YOUR GRAIN GROW A PENIS!" Having uttered his curse, the Lama went on his way.

At harvest time, the couple went to their field. What they saw shocked them. It was filled with a crop of penises. They began crying because of what had happened to them. Not only were they terribly embarrassed, but, since that was their only field, they would not have any grain to live on for the next year.

Naturally, so strange a story spread to villages near and far. It happened that Uncle Tompa also heard about this weird crop and he came to see. The poor couple's field was filled with

unbelievable penises in all sizes, like mushrooms protruding from the ground. He saw immediately that the couple had a most lucrative crop on their hands.

He went to the couple's home, where he found them crying and rolling on the floor in grief. They could not bear the terrible disaster. Uncle consoled them. "No, no. Don't worry so much; I'll sell them for you and from that you'll be able to buy more grain than you would have gotten from the field."

The couple thanked Uncle Tompa for his comforting words and kind offer. Uncle asked them to bring donkeys with many empty sacks to load all the penises. They started harvesting the penises by unplugging them from the ground and loaded them on the donkeys just as Uncle had asked them to do. But the couple still did not know what Uncle had in mind or where he was going with this embarrassing crop.

Uncle Tompa left the couple's house and promised he would return in a few days. Then Uncle went directly to one of Tibet's largest nunneries with his donkeys.

As soon as he arrived in the nunnery's open courtyard, he unloaded the donkeys and let them out of the yard. He put down a few big pieces of cloth and arranged all the penises in rows according to their size. As soon as he was through, he shouted, "ANY ONE WHO WANTS A MAGIC PENIS TO FULFILL ALL SEXUAL DESIRES CAN PURCHASE ONE RIGHT NOW!" He shouted again and again. But he did not attract any customers until dark.

The Abbess of the nunnery was the first one to come out and she asked Uncle, "What's your price for the biggest one over there?" She pointed to it while coyly covering her mouth. Uncle asked a great deal of money for it, but she did not mind paying the whole amount. Holding it in her hand, she asked him, "How do I use this?"

Uncle warned, "Well, you have to keep it away from dogs

and cats because they might eat it." Then he carefully instructed her, "When you want to enjoy yourself, simply say 'Tsk, tsk, tsk!' This Magic Penis will come and screw you until you take a long deep breath and sigh, 'Hu!'"

The Abbess was very happy to have such a useful object in her life. Because, as everybody knows, nuns are not allowed to enjoy men.

After the Abbess left in great excitement, almost all the nuns came and bought the remaining penises. Uncle was very busy pricing them according to size and collecting the money. He also had to give the other nuns careful instructions on how to use them. Before long, he had sold his entire stock.

When he had sold the last one, he fetched the donkeys and went back to the couple. They were astounded to see Uncle Tompa with such a large sum of money. Now they could buy everything they needed, far more than they could have gotten for their grain. The happy couple went off to look for the holy Lama to get him to put a magic curse on their field every year.

In the meantime, the Abbess followed the instructions given her by Uncle Tompa. She called, "Tsk, tsk, tsk!" Sure enough, the penis jumped on her and humped her. When she wanted it to stop, she gave out a long sigh, "Hu!" and the penis would fall out. The Abbess enjoyed herself and loved the Magic Penis so much that she had a special silver box made in which she kept it wrapped in silk. She felt it was so precious in her life that she would never spend a night without it. The Abbess and the Magic Penis became inseparable.

Years passed. One day she was invited to a special ceremony by a rich family who lived a long distance away. The Abbess forgot to bring the silver box with her. She would have to stay there several days to perform the rituals. The first night without her Magic Penis made her very grumpy and unhappy. The next day she told the family she did not want to stay for the whole ceremony. She explained that she must return to the nunnery that very day, because she had left a special holy object there without which, according to her religious vows, she was not allowed to spend the night.

After she had told all these lies to the family, they still insisted she stay to complete the ritual. They suggested they send their servant to pick it up. If he rode a horse both ways, he could go and come back that same day.

The Abbess finally agreed. She told the servant, "There's a silver box under my bed. You must not open it. If you do, you'll be committing a great sin!" The servant promised to obey her.

He went to the nunnery, picked up the silver box, and started back. Along the way, he wondered, "What can there be in such a precious box?" He wanted to look inside, but was afraid he might commit a sin. After some distance, he came to a place where there was nobody around. He got down from his horse and rested for a while.

Soon his curiosity about what was in the silver box got the better of him, his fear of sinning abandoned him and he opened it. What he saw was something large and thick, shaped like a cylinder, wrapped in silk. He unwrapped the silk and uncovered the huge penis. Awestruck by the sight of it, he clucked in amazement, "Tsk, tsk, tsk!"

Immediately, the penis jumped on him and looked for a hole. Since he was a male, the penis could only find one hole; it drilled in and start to screw. The poor servant was terrified. He cried out and aimlessly ran every which way until he was absolutely exhausted. Finally he breathed a long sigh, "Hu," and out the penis fell.

The servant got very angry and shouted every swearword he knew at the dreaded penis. He picked up a big rock and beat it until it was mashed and flattened out of shape. Then he wrapped it up in the same silk, put it back in the silver box, and continued on his way.

As soon as he arrived, he handed the box to the Abbess, saying he had not committed any sin. The Abbess was very happy to have it back with her. When night fell, she went to bed and called, "Tsk, tsk, tsk!" But the penis did not come to her as usual. She called again and again, but still it did not come. She suspected something had happened to it, so she opened the silver box and found her beloved penis beaten completely flat. All night long she could not bear the sadness of what had happened to her lover, but she could not tell anyone because it would have been humiliating for a nun.

The next morning, she woke up in a very sad mood. The family wanted to know what had happened to her. She told them that she was very ill. The family brought in a physician to examine her. Instead, without saying anything, the Abbess put the beaten penis on a plate and set it in front of him to see if he could examine it and bring it back to life.

The physician thought that he had been served some kind of beaten meat dish. So, he ate it. The Abbess died from shock.

Uncle Tompa
Becomes a Nun

Uncle Tompa had a very smooth face that could almost pass for a woman's. He had thought for a long time he would like to screw some fresh young virgin nuns at a nunnery. So he traveled around looking for one to join. He finally found one with hundreds of nuns and, donning nun's robes, he went to see the Abbess. The Abbess allowed the newly arrived 'nun' to enter her nunnery.

Uncle had been there several months, when suddenly many of the nuns started becoming pregnant, even though the nunnery was well protected from men coming in at night. In spite of the restrictions, the number of pregnancies kept increasing. The teachers and leaders of the nunnery paid still closer attention to see if any man was coming in at night, but they could not find anyone.

The leaders began to suspect that there must be a man amongst the nuns. They would have to find out who it was. It would not be an easy task to examine every nun's bottom because there were so many.

So the leaders built two thick walls, one next to the other. All the nuns were told to jump, one by one, from one wall to the other, while the leaders looked up from the ground to see if any of the nuns had a penis. This way they could find out who was the cause of all the pregnancies. Since Uncle could not escape the inspection, he tied his long penis with a string, pulled it

back between his legs, and tied it up tight to his waist belt. Then Uncle joined the jumping with the rest of the nuns.

Uncle's turn came. He jumped and was passed. The leaders could not detect any difference between him and the other nuns. So everybody jumped again. Still, they could not find the man.

The leaders ordered everyone to jump a third time. When Uncle's turn came, he jumped, but this time the string broke loose and his penis fell, dangling down. The leaders suddenly saw it. They seized him and realized he must be the man who had been sleeping with all the young nuns!

They tied up his arms, took off all his robes and marched him around the nunnery in a large procession, showing all that he was the one who caused the pregnancies. Then they put Uncle in a dark room without food and tied his arms and legs to a thick pillar. This was the worst kind of torture they could think of.

Later on, the leaders eavesdropped on him to hear what Uncle was saying to himself. Uncle knew this, so he muttered again and again, "Ah! The Lord has blessed me! I'm perfectly comfortable being tied up like this, but it would be horrible torture if they took some wet cow hide strips smeared with butter, and tied up my arms and legs with them." The nuns behind the door thought, "That must be a very painful torture for him." So they brought wet cow hide strips with butter smeared on them and tied up his arms and legs.

Naturally, the butter on the wet cow hide made it very slippery, and the water made it stretch. Early the next morning, he slipped out of his bonds, jumped from the window, and ran away without any clothes.

As soon as he was further down the trail, he met a man riding a horse with two saddlebags full of food. Uncle Tompa asked him, "Where are you going?"

"I'm going to see my sister at the nunnery," he answered.

"Don't you know the nunnery just made a new rule that any man who goes there can enter only if he's naked? See, I just walked in and out without any clothes."

Hearing this, and seeing that Uncle was naked, the poor man thought, "That must be true!" So he asked Uncle, "Could you please watch my horse and things?" Of course, Uncle said yes, and reminded him not to take too long. The man took off his clothes and went to the nunnery.

As soon as he walked into the courtyard, a whole army of nuns emerged from their rooms, jumped on him and beat him up. Some believed he was Uncle, and some thought he was just trying to insult them. Finally they stopped beating him and asked why he had come in without his clothes. He told them about meeting the naked man and what the man had said about the nunnery's new rule.

The nuns rushed into the room where they had tied Uncle up, but Uncle Tompa was gone. They dressed the man in nun's clothes because that was all they had. Then they went down to the place where the man had met Uncle to see if he was still there. But he and all the man's belongings were gone.

Many months passed. One day, by accident, the man ran into Uncle in Lhasa. On seeing him, Uncle immediately grabbed hold of a very tall religious pillar which stands right in the center of Lhasa. He looked intently at the top of the monument. The man came up to Uncle and shouted, "You're a liar and a thief! You robbed my horse and everything I had!"

Uncle Tompa kept looking at the top of the religious pillar and said, "Ah! I've been looking for you to return your horse and goods, but the Tibetan Government has appointed me Religious Pillar Watcher to see that this monument doesn't fall down, so I didn't have time."

The man said, "Well, I'll take your place as Religious Pillar

Watcher if you just go and bring me my horse and things!"

Uncle instructed him, "All right. Just remember! It's very important to shout if you see the pillar start to fall down." The man agreed to do so. He grabbed the pillar, which was eleven stories high, and Uncle went away.

The man clung fast to the pillar. Soon there were clouds flying overhead in the clear sky. They were moving very fast. The poor man, looking at the moving clouds above the pillar, thought the monument was falling down. So he shouted over and over, "People of Lhasa! The Religious Pillar is falling down!"

Everybody looked at him and soon he found himself in the center of a big crowd. Everyone thought, "He's making such an inauspicious noise. He's trying to disturb us and insulting our Religious Pillar with his lies."

So they all beat him up, and when they were finished, the police came and arrested him for disturbing the peace and causing a riot.

Uncle Tompa
Becomes the Bride
of a Rich Man

ne day Uncle Tompa went on a business trip to another part of Tibet. But he had no success and became very distraught. He wandered off to a different village. As he was entering the village, he heard some people talking about how the richest and cruelest man there was looking for a woman to marry. Hearing this, Uncle made further inquiries. He decided that to see if he could cheat this person.

Since he had a very smooth face, it was easy for Uncle to dress up like a woman. He bought the lung of a sheep and tied it up between his thighs with a very strong string to cover his penis. Then he cut an opening in the lung to make it look just like a vagina.

Uncle appeared as a pretty lady from a different village. He rented a house next door to that rich man's home, so that the man would see him. The next day Uncle, dressed up in fancy clothes, looked out of the window to see when the rich man was coming. Soon the rich man came riding up on a horse and passed by Uncle's window. He suddenly saw a beautiful woman, whom he had never seen before, gazing down at him.

So he stopped his horse and stared up at her. Uncle stared back with a sexy gaze. The rich man asked her where she came from and what her name was. He immediately fell in love with

37

this new 'lady'. That night he came over to sleep with her and had a beautiful sexual experience with the sheep's lung.

The next day the rich man decided to marry the new 'lady.' But Uncle refused to marry him unless he gave him all the expensive jewelry that he could afford. That was no problem for the rich man. He brought a great deal of gold, turquoise, diamonds, and all kinds of expensive baubles to please his bride.

The following day the wedding started. All the people of the village came to join in the festivities. The rich man was very happy to have such a new beautiful bride. The second day was the wedding reception. Everybody was enjoying themselves and were happy that a new bride from a different place had come to live with them. Uncle wore all the expensive jewelry and clothing that the man had given him. That day he took off the sheep's lung that had been tied between his thighs to cover his penis, which the rich man had been humping for the last several days.

All of a sudden, Uncle appeared in the reception crowd, dancing around and openly holding his own thick, large penis. Everybody at the reception was astonished and shocked to see the bride had a penis. Then Uncle jumped onto a horse that was in the yard and rode away with all the valuable jewelry and clothing.

The groom was so shocked at what had happened that he hid himself in a very dark room for many days, ashamed to show his face to anyone.

Uncle Tompa returned to his village loaded with jewelry and fine clothing, and told everyone what a success his business trip had been.

Uncle Tompa
Reads Holy Scripture

Tibetans are highly devoted to Buddhism. Most families invite a Lama or a good reader of Buddhist scriptures once a month, or at least once every year, to their homes to read. Uncle Tompa was a good scripture reader. People often invited him to read to insure good luck and prosperity for their families. One day he was invited to read a scripture which normally takes several days.

The father of this family had not a single strand of hair on his head. For this reason he was always ashamed to go out to any public gathering and stayed home all the time. When he absolutely had to go out, he would wear a special head cover.

Uncle Tompa spent a few days reading the holy scriptures at the family's house. But the family did not serve Uncle good food. The obligation of any host is to serve the reader especially good meals, and offer an amount of money after he completes reciting the holy scriptures. At that family's home he was served only hardly edible beans. The food they served him was fit only for a dog, Uncle Tompa thought. They never served him any meat, so Uncle was very unhappy.

He noticed the family had several sheep, one black and the rest white. The black sheep kept on charging Uncle, butting him any time he went out. While the father of the family, the bald-headed man, was intently listening to the holy scriptures, Uncle devised a plan.

The man himself was unable to read or write. All he knew about the scriptures was that which was read to him. So Uncle made up words of his own, pretending this was what the scriptures said. He recited very loudly:

IF ONE HAS NO STRANDS OF HAIR ON THE HEAD,
ONE WILL HAVE HAIR GROWN SOON,
IF HE WEARS THE WARM SKIN OF A BLACK SHEEP.

Hearing this, the man jumped up in surprise and asked, "What! Is this true?"

"Yes, of course it's true," Uncle answered, "The Lord says so!"

The poor man believed it, and sent someone out to kill the black sheep. He took the skin while it was still warm and put it on his head. Uncle was served mutton for lunch and dinner.

The poor bald-headed man kept wearing the skin. After a few days, the skin started smelling bad, so once again Uncle made up words and recited loudly:

IF ONE WEARS THE SKIN OF A BLACK SHEEP
ON THE HEAD LONGER THAN ONE SUNSET,
NOTHING WILL GROW ON THE HEAD."

Hearing these holy words, the man said to Uncle, "What? Read that again!"

So Uncle read it over and explained, "The Lord says, if one wears the skin longer than one sunset, no hair will grow on his head. So, since you've been wearing it for quite a few sunsets, it looks like you're out of luck."

The poor man believed him and threw the skin away, while Uncle Tompa continued reading.

UNCLE TOMPA
Sleeps with a Virgin

ibetan families often invite weavers into their homes to weave for them. Uncle Tompa was very good at weaving woolen fabrics for making clothes. Once Uncle Tompa was invited to a family where there was only a mother and her daughter. The daughter was a virgin and very pretty.

Uncle had been weaving for several days. He tried to seduce the virgin girl a few times, but could not manage it. At last he figured out a way.

While Uncle was sitting at his loom weaving in the entrance of the house, he noticed the girl walking downstairs to go to the bathroom. As soon as he saw her, he sped up his weaving. When the girl saw how fast he was weaving, she asked him, "Why are you in such a hurry?"

Uncle replied, "Well, I have to go to the bathroom, but I must finish this yarn before I go, that's why."

Uncle asked her, as he continued working very quickly, "Where are you going?"

She replied, "I'm going to the bathroom."

"Since you're going to the bathroom, could you please take my urine with you?"

She thought and then answered, "Why not?" So Uncle asked her to take off her clothes and then he had sex with her.

As soon as he was through, Uncle continued his weaving, and the girl went to the bathroom, thinking she was taking Uncle's urine for him. Then she went to help her mother in the kitchen. She told her the whole story about the favor she had done for Uncle Tompa.

As soon as her mother heard the impossible story of Uncle's trick, she yelled, "No! No! How can anyone send his urine through someone else? He did not send his urine, he screwed you, that's what he did!"

The girl thought, "That's right; that must be so! I must go and yell at him!"

So she went back to Uncle and shouted, "You didn't give me your urine, you humped me!"

Uncle said, "No! No! I really did send my urine with you." The argument went on for a while, then suddenly Uncle said, "If you're that concerned about it, let me have my urine back so you don't have to be so worried!"

The girl thought, "It would be better if I returned his urine; then I'll be clean." She said, "Yes, why don't you take it back?"

So Uncle took her clothes off and had sex with her once again.

Uncle Tompa
Plants Human Hair

ncle Tompa was not rich; he was always short of something. One day he was expecting some guests to come that evening, but he had no butter to put in the tea, nor could he afford to buy any. Tibetan tea is always made with butter.

In Tibetan houses butter is stored in water containers to keep it fresh and cool. Uncle Tompa looked through his window into his neighbor's kitchen. In his neighbor's water tank he saw a big ball of butter, and he thought, "How can I get this butter for my guests?"

The head of the family next door was bald. He was always ashamed of going to parties or any other public gathering because he had not one single strand of hair on his head. That morning Uncle saw the bald-headed man sitting in the sun just in front of his house. So Uncle took a sharp awl in one hand and a bunch of black yak-tail hair and walked by him pretending to be in a hurry.

Seeing Uncle, the man asked, "Hey, where are you going in such a hurry?"

"I met someone like you, a bald-headed person. He asked me to plant hair on his head, so I'm going there," Uncle answered.

"Wait, wait! Can you plant human hair?"

"Of course. Didn't you know it could be done?"

"Can you plant it on me as well?" the man asked.

"Yes, yes! Why don't I do you first?" Uncle replied.

Uncle had him wash his head and took him into the house. There he began stabbing his head with the awl. "Oh! Ah!" the man cried out, "It really hurts!"

Uncle agreed. "Oh! Yes, yes. It's not so easy to plant hair; you'll just have to bear the pain."

Soon Uncle was stabbing away continuously, and each place where he stabbed, he put one strand of yak hair to show him he was really planting hair. Uncle Tompa stabbed him many times. Soon the bald man could absolutely bear the pain no longer and tears ran down his cheeks.

Finally Uncle said, "Well, if you don't want the hair planted, I'll release you from our agreement if you give me a ball of butter." The man decided to give him the butter he had in the water container and give up this miserable hair-planting business.

Uncle took the butter and went away.

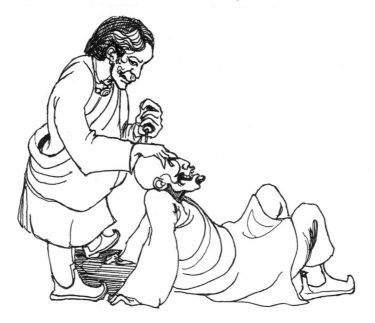

UNCLE TOMPA
Paints a Bull

ne day Uncle Tompa was walking through the fields. He saw a man plowing. His plow was being pulled by a pair of bulls. Uncle saw that one of the bulls was black, while the other was white-and-black spotted. Uncle sat down near the man and said, "Hello! You have a very healthy pair of bulls. It's too bad they're an unmatched pair."

"Why is that?" the man asked.

"Because one is black and the other is spotted."

"There's nothing I can do about that."

"Sure you can! You can make the spotted one into a black one."

"Could you do that for me then?"

"Yes, yes, and it'll cost you only one cup of Chang beer," Uncle replied.

The man agreed on the price. Then Uncle untied the spotted bull from the plow. He brought some black mud and rubbed it all over the bull's body. Finally, the white spots were all covered with mud and it looked as black as the other bull. Uncle gave it to the owner and said, "After three days, give him a bath and then all the spots will turn as black as they are now."

The man continued his plowing and said, "You can go to my house for the beer." Uncle went to his house which was not too far from where he was plowing.

Uncle met the owner's wife and said, "I just sold a black bull to your husband. He told me to get the money from you. If you don't trust me, you can look out the window and see for yourself." She looked down from her window and saw the pair of black bulls with which her husband was plowing. So she gave Uncle the cost of one bull and Uncle went off with the money.

Uncle Tompa
Drops Shit in the King's Lap

nce there were many kings in different regions of Tibet. Uncle Tompa happened to be a good friend of one of these kings, and so he got a job as his secretary. The king himself was not able to write or read, but he was highly devoted to Buddhism.

At first, Uncle made the king very happy with his work, but one day he annoyed him greatly. The king decided to punish him. He made Uncle take off all the clothes he was wearing and put him on the palace roof during the coldest time of the year. Poor Uncle suffered from the cold all night long.

Early the next morning, Uncle scraped off some of the white lime used to whitewash the palace wall. Soon he had enough to spread out on the floor. Then he shit on the white lime dust, picked up a stick and stabbed it into the shit. It soon froze because of the cold. He picked up the stick which now had the frozen shit on it and a white bottom from the lime. He wrote some words on the bottom.

Uncle looked down through the skylight into the king's private chapel and saw him sitting cross- legged, meditating before a splendid altar of Buddha and all the gods. Uncle dropped his shit through the skylight right onto the king's lap.

The king woke up in surprise from his meditation. When he looked at the strange object more carefully, he saw there was some writing on the bottom.

Since he could not read, he ordered his servants to bring Uncle down into his presence. Uncle, still shivering from the cold, was served a hot breakfast.

Soon after, the king ordered Uncle to read the "Miracle Shit." Uncle bowed down three times in respect and sat below the king's throne in a very humble posture. He picked up the shit and read the writing on the bottom very loudly:

WOODEN HANDLED AND WHITE BOTTOMED,
THIS IS SHIT FROM HEAVEN.
HE IS THE LUCKIEST KING
WHEN IT DROPS IN HIS LAP!

Uncle stood up in amazement and said, "Ah! You are very fortunate because this is shit from heaven, and whoever it drops on is the luckiest person on earth. You should eat a little bit of it to get its blessings."

The king touched it to his forehead, ate a piece of it, and put the rest on his altar. Uncle Tompa saluted and was dismissed.

UNCLE TOMPA
Becomes a Porter

Uncle Tompa was down to his last penny when he decided to go out and make some money. So he went to Lhasa and took a long rope with him. When he arrived, he looked around and saw some porters waiting for work to come by. Uncle sat down and waited with them. After a while a man came and shouted to the porters, including Uncle, "I have a box full of china to carry home from here. Whoever carries it for me will get three pieces of good advice for his wages!"

Hearing this, all the porters ignored him. But Uncle thought to himself, "Something like money can be earned any time, but good advice is always hard to come by!" So Uncle said to the man, "I'll carry it for you."

They both agreed on the deal, and Uncle carried his box full of fragile china. After some distance, Uncle asked him, "Would you please give me one piece of advice now?"

The man said, "Don't believe anybody who tells you it's better to go hungry than to eat your fill!"

"That's good advice." They walked some distance and again Uncle asked, "How about giving me the second piece of advice?"

The man said, "Don't believe anybody who tells you it's better to go on foot than to ride a horse!"

"That's true and good advice." They continued their walk and came to the door of the man's house. Uncle asked, "Now could you give me your third piece of advice?"

"Don't believe anybody who tells you there are porters who are more foolish than you." All of a sudden Uncle let go of the rope that was tied to the box. It fell to the ground and everything shattered.

Uncle said to the man, "Don't believe anybody who tells you none of your china is broken!"

UNCLE TOMPA
Tries to Carry a Boulder

nce a rich peasant had a fertile field. At the center of the field sat a big boulder, which was impossible to move. Uncle Tompa was running out of food, so he wondered how he could cheat the rich land owner. As he walked by, he saw the rock, went over to the owner and said, "Why don't you remove the rock that's blocking so much of your field?"

The rich man replied, "I want to, but I can't."

Uncle said, "I'll remove it for you."

"Could you?" asked the man with surprise.

"Yes, yes! But you must hire twenty strong young people to put it on my back, and I need a great length of rope."

The rich man agreed to that. The next day the man came to call on Uncle after hiring twenty young people and buying a long piece of rope.

Uncle had breakfast and spent some time talking to the owner.

When it was time for lunch, Uncle said, "Why don't you serve me lunch so I don't have to come back for food until dinner?" They served him lunch.

Uncle kept talking with them until it was time for a tea break. Uncle said, "Why don't you serve me tea now, so I don't have to come back for it?"

Once more Uncle kept talking to the owner and his family until dinnertime. Uncle asked them to serve him dinner, so they did that as well.

Then Uncle said, "Why don't you give me my wages for today so I don't have to come back to bother you for it?" The family did not see anything wrong with that, so they gave him one day's salary.

It was getting rather dark. Finally Uncle got up and asked for the rope. Then he and the twenty young people went out to the field. When they arrived, Uncle tied the long rope around the rock. Uncle held the rope and leaned his back against one side of the boulder and asked the twenty young people to push and load the rock onto him.

He said, "All right, PUSH! PUSH!" They tried and tried, but it was impossible for them to get the rock to shake even one inch, much less lift it onto Uncle's back.

Uncle shouted, "Let's try again!" They still could not move it.

Uncle said to the landowner, "These people are too weak to load the rock onto me. If they had loaded it on my back, I could have carried it away. These people have failed their assignment." Then Uncle went home.

Uncle Tompa
Borrows a Pot
from a Rich Man

nce again, Uncle Tompa wanted to cheat some rich people. One day he went to a notoriously stingy rich man and borrowed a large copper pot, something which is highly valued in Tibet.

"How kind this stingy man is to Uncle," the neighbors thought, after they saw him walking out of the rich man's house with his big copper pot.

After some time, Uncle Tompa returned to the rich man's house. As soon as he walked into the room, he said, "Congratulations to you! Congratulations to you! How fortunate you are!"

"What for?" the man asked.

"Your big pot has given birth to a gorgeous little son. Isn't that a piece of good news?"

"Nonsense! How can a pot give birth to a son?" the rich man challenged.

Now, Uncle had already brought with him a tiny pot, exactly the same shape as the bigger one he had borrowed, wrapped in a cloth. He opened the cloth and showed the little pot. "If you don't believe me, just look here! What do you call this?" he asked cheerfully.

No matter how serious Uncle looked, the rich man refused to believe him. He thought to himself, "If Uncle is such a fool, it would be silly of me not to take advantage of him!" He then

acted as if he were very happy to have the new son of his pot and he said, "Thank you for your congratulations on this splendid occasion! How's his mother doing?"

Uncle put the small copper pot into the rich man's hand and again told him what a beautiful son his pot had given birth to. "The little son really looks like his mother, doesn't he?" mused Uncle.

"Yes, yes," the man agreed.

Then Uncle took his leave. The rich man said, "From now on, take good care of the mother, my big copper pot! May she have more sons like this one in the future!"

A few days later, Uncle came back to the rich man. He was on the verge of tears and he sadly announced, "Something terrible has happened to us!"

"What happened?" the man asked with surprise.

"Your big copper pot is dead."

The rich man shouted, "Nonsense! How can a pot die?"

Uncle replied, "If a big pot can give birth to a son, then why can't it die?"

Naturally the rich man did not feel like letting Uncle have the big pot just like that. He said, "Well, anyway, since my big pot is dead, will you please bring its corpse back to me?"

"Sorry! I've already cremated it."

"Where was it cremated?" he roared.

"In the blacksmith's forge," was the answer.

Outraged at Uncle Tompa, the rich man knew he was being cheated and he could not conceal his anger. "You're a robber; you robbed my big pot!" he shouted.

Uncle shouted back at him, "You're the robber who robbed my small pot!" They started to quarrel. All the neighbors came to see what was happening. But since the rich man feared he would get a bad reputation, he stopped arguing about his pot, walked back into his house and shut the door.

UNCLE TOMPA's
Wife Dies

ncle Tompa's nag of a wife died after a long illness. The same morning he cried and cried, saying, "I shall not remain very long, either! I shall not remain a very long time!"

The villagers thought, "Oh! poor Uncle! He's saying he also wants to die soon." So everybody from the village brought food and Chang beer to console him, saying, "It's too bad your wife has died, but may you live a long life."

By evening, with all the food and Chang, he was drunk. He laughed, sang songs and danced around. The villagers were shocked. They asked him, "What's happened to you? This morning you were saying you wouldn't remain too long; but now you're laughing and dancing and singing songs!"

Uncle replied, "Well, I meant that I would not remain long in mourning. I didn't mean I was going to die. My mourning didn't last. It's gone, right? Now I'm going to enjoy myself."

UNCLE TOMPA
Plays a Trick
on His New Wife

ome time later, after Uncle Tompa's first wife died, he married another woman, with whom he lived for many years. Uncle's new wife was a pretty woman who liked to sleep with different men. He had known this for some time. Once, when Uncle had to go away on business, he thought of playing a trick on her to make her stop.

It took quite a while before Uncle could think up a scheme. One day Uncle was called by the governor of a different region to come there and weave fabrics for his family, since Uncle was very good at that. He left his wife at home and went to the other region.

Uncle spent a few months at that place making fabrics. The governor was very pleased with his work and asked, "Do you want to come to settle here? I'll give you work as long as you remain here."

Uncle showed some interest but said, "Well, Your Lordship! I'd very much like to move here, but there's a problem which must first be solved. Perhaps you can help."

"What's that?"

Uncle replied, "My wife is a very pretty woman, so many men like to sleep with her. But whoever sleeps with her gets killed except me!"

"Why is it so?"

"My wife has something very unusual. A snake lives in her asshole and it comes out and bites whoever makes love to her! That snake has already killed several people in my village, so I'm afraid it will happen here too!"

The governor said, "I'll gather my people and warn them. That should convince them not to bother her."

Uncle agreed and decided to move there. Soon after, Uncle went back to his village to pick up his wife and possessions. While he was gone, the governor called the people together and issued a decree that no one should sleep with Uncle's wife.

When Uncle returned home, he told his wife that they were moving to a new village, where it was much easier to make a living. As they continued talking, he suddenly laughed and said, "Do you know what a strange thing all the men have there?"

"No, what's that?"

"All the men there have double penises!"

His wife would not believe him and wanted to see for herself.

Finally they moved to the new village. Because of his work, Uncle often had to go out and could not return home at night. His wife had to stay home alone. Many of the young men fell in love with her and wanted to have sex, but they were all afraid they would get bitten by her snake and be killed.

One night, while Uncle was away, a young foolhardy man wanted to sleep with her. He devised a way to avoid getting killed by her snake. He and some friends went to her house carrying a thick long rope. They climbed onto the roof, tied one end of the rope around the man's waist and lowered him down into her room through the skylight. This way, when the snake started to crawl out of her asshole, he could shout to the others to pull him back up quickly, and not get bitten. She was very glad to see him. They went to bed right away and started screwing.

Uncle's wife was lying on her back. While they were humping she was thinking, "Now, my husband told me that all the men here have double penises, but it feels like this man has only one!" So she reached her hand around and under her thigh and started feeling to see if she could find the second penis.

When he felt her fingers moving up from behind, he yelled desperately, "Pull! Pull! The snake! The snake is coming out!" The men on the roof jerked the rope up so fast that he hit his head on the edge of the skylight. He broke his neck and was killed instantly.

The next day all the people in the village were talking about the man who got killed by Uncle's snake. From then on, Uncle enjoyed his wife without interference from other visitors.

UNCLE TOMPA
Makes the King
Bark like a Dog

I t was the first day of the Tibetan New Year. Everybody was busy celebrating. According to tradition, one member of each family must go to see their king with offerings, such as Tibetan breads, fruits, fabrics, and white scarves for good luck.

Uncle Tompa told everyone there that he could make the king bark like a dog on this occasion, but nobody believed him. "He won't do that. It's too inauspicious." But Uncle promised that he would.

That whole day the king was busy receiving his people for the New Year's greetings. The king was sitting on his throne wearing his most expensive clothes and crown. Many people were sitting down having a meal with him. All of a sudden the king saw Uncle Tompa rush in.

The king asked Uncle, "Where have you been all this time? You're normally the first one here."

Uncle said, "My lord! There was an outstandingly beautiful dog for sale. I was trying to buy it as a present for you."

In Tibet dogs are judged by the strength of their barking, as well as by their appearance. So the king asked, "What does the dog sound like?"

Uncle made a sound just like a cat. "Meow, Meow!"

The king shook his head and exclaimed, "That's not the sound of an outstanding dog. That sounds just like a cat!"

"My lord, what does a good dog sound like then?" Uncle Tompa asked curiously.

The king put his hands on the table in front of the throne. He stood up on all fours just like a dog and barked, "Woof! Woof! Woof!"

Everyone laughed at how Uncle Tompa's trick had worked. In Tibet people think that to bark on New Year's Day is horribly inauspicious. Discreetly, his people called him "The Barking King."

Uncle Tompa
Travels as the King's Servant

 king from a far away state had to go to Lhasa, the capital of Tibet, for a conference. Of course, high-ranking persons never travel alone, so he brought Uncle along as his servant. While the king rode a horse, poor Uncle had to walk behind him carrying a heavy load of blankets and pots for cooking along the way. The king was also very stingy. He ate all the good food while Uncle had to eat his leftovers.

Even after they had reached Lhasa, the king continued to treat Uncle very badly. On the day the king went to the conference, before he left, he put his best Tsampa, the barley flour that is Tibet's staple food, in one pot and some boiled eggs in another. Pointing to the pot of Tsampa, the king said, "You mustn't eat this tsampa! It's poisoned." Then he pointed to the pot of eggs and said, "And you should not open this pot. It's full of birds and if you open it, they'll all fly off."

Uncle knew the king was only trying to keep the best food for himself, but he pretended he didn't know anything. As soon as the king left for the conference, Uncle ate up all the Tsampa and eggs. He had a good lunch for the first time on the journey.

That evening when the king walked in, Uncle pretended to tremble with fright. The king opened the pots of Tsampa and eggs and found them both empty. He became very angry and screamed at Uncle, "What happened to the birds and poisoned Tsampa?"

Uncle replied, "The birds were making so much noise that I thought they needed a bit of fresh air. So I opened the lid a little, but they all flew away. I was so worried that I wanted to kill myself. So I ate up all the poisoned Tsampa. But unfortunately, my lord, I didn't die!"

Uncle Tompa
and the Stingy King

undreds of years ago in Tibet, there were many small kingdoms ruled over by local kings and queens. While some were very pious and kind to their subjects, some oppressed and ruled their subjects cruelly.

Many of those kings were illiterate. So they always hired someone who could read and write for them. Since Uncle Tompa was literate, he was hired by a local king to do the job. This king turned out be one of the cruelest to his people. He was so stingy, he would even measure out the water people drank from his well.

One day, Uncle Tompa went out and gathered all the heads of the families. He told them that he was going to make the king give a most memorable and lavish party for the entire kingdom.

They all laughed at Uncle Tompa for his ridiculous wishful thinking and asked, "Does the wolf ever let a drop of blood fall from its mouth? Does the sun ever rise from the west?" They shook their heads in disbelief and walked away

Uncle Tompa shouted behind them, "You'll be invited shortly."

He returned to the palace, and went directly to the well where the palace got its water supply. The well was within view of the palace and the king often went up to the rooftop balcony to gaze out. Uncle Tompa looked into the well and pretended as if he were talking to someone there. It happened that king was on the balcony looking out, and he saw Uncle Tompa, who seemed to be arguing with someone in the well.

Noticing that the king was looking at him, Uncle Tompa started to shout. He pointed his finger into the well and swung his arms up and down furiously. Since the well was some distance away, the king couldn't hear what was being said.

A short time later, Uncle Tompa returned to the king, acting as if he had been in a grave argument, shaking his head in disbelief. The king immediately inquired, "Whom were you talking to?"

With a serious expression, Uncle said, "I was drawing some water from the well, and suddenly a woman Naga, the spirit of the well, appeared. She claimed that she's the owner of the water. She was holding the largest gold nugget that I've ever seen. It was about the size of your head!"

When the king heard this, he was instantly filled with envy and asked, "Why were you arguing with her?"

"You won't believe what she said about you." He paused momentarily, then continued, "She said that you're the stingiest person who ever lived on earth. I retorted that it was not true and told her that you're the most generous person who's ever lived."

The king smiled with gratification and asked, "What does she want me to do to prove it?"

Uncle announced, "She said if you can throw the most lavish three-day party for the entire kingdom, she'll split the cost with you fifty-fifty. If she fails to do so, she'll gladly offer the gold to you."

When the king heard this, his eyes glowed with greed for the gold. Uncle Tompa continued, "If you fail to give the party, she said she's going to move her water away and this well will go dry."

Hearing this offer, the king wasted no time. He summoned

all his servants and ordered them to prepare the largest and most lavish party in history. He sent his servants to every door inviting each household to attend. Everyone knew their stingy king had been tricked by Uncle Tompa.

The party was thrown at the palace. People ate, drank Chang beer, sang songs, danced and played dice, making merry for three days. Meanwhile, Uncle Tompa was staggering around drunk, laughing, and asking the heads of the families, "Isn't there a wolf who lets blood drop from his mouth? Hasn't the sun risen in the west today?" They were all amazed by this rascal's cleverness.

After three days, the king was more than eager to send Uncle Tompa to the well to retrieve the gold. He knew the Naga lady of the well had failed to provide her equal share for the party. The king ordered Uncle Tompa to go to the well and bring him the gold nugget. The king himself went to the balcony to watch.

When Uncle got to the well he looked in and started calling and beckoning. He pretended to talk, gesticulating all the while. Soon he acted angry, shouting, pointing his finger, throwing his arms in the air in a rage, stomping his feet on the ground. Shortly, he started walking back, fuming with anger, shaking his head in disbelief.

The king went to meet him and asked, "Where's my gold?"

"The Naga lady wouldn't give it to you, because she said that she provided her share for the party."

The king became furious and shouted, "No! She didn't provide a thing."

Uncle Tompa said, "That's what I said, but she said that she provided her water to cook the food for the party. Then she disappeared into the water."

The king, still infuriated, could not believe what Uncle Tompa had said. He went to the well himself and called the Naga lady over and over, but no one appeared.

OTHER TALES

The Village Fool

nce upon a time a fool lived in a village. He thought he should go to the city, thinking he would be the brightest, smartest, and most handsome man there. He expected everyone would come to admire him. That day he dressed up like a rich person and started his journey.

When he arrived in the city, he came to a shop where they sold all kinds of vegetables. He looked around, saw some pumpkins, and wondered what they could be. He finally decided they must be the eggs of a horse. So he asked the shopkeeper, "Hello! Are those horse's eggs?"

The shopkeeper thought, "What a stupid person! I'll give his foolish question a foolish answer." So he replied, "Yes sir, they're horse eggs."

The fool asked, "How much are they?"

The shopkeeper wanted fifty cents, although pumpkins normally cost only one cent. And sure enough, he was willing to pay that much for the 'horse egg.'

After purchasing it he headed back towards his village. He thought, "It was lucky that I was able to buy such a marvelous thing in town! I'll wrap the 'horse egg' in warm clothes and keep it by the side of the oven where it's warm. Then after some time, the egg will hatch, and I'll have a colt. When the horse gets big, I'll sell it for a good price, and out of that money I'll buy several more eggs from the same shop. But I'd better not tell anyone in the village, because they'll also learn how to get horses this way."

Making all kinds of imaginary plans along the way, he came to a small pool with a tree growing beside it, just outside his village. It was a rather hot day, so he decided to take a bath before he got home. He put his 'horse egg' between two branches of the tree, took off his clothes, jumped in the pool, and enjoyed his bath.

All of a sudden, the wind blew, and his 'horse egg' fell down from the tree and broke in pieces. Now there just happened to be a rabbit sleeping by the tree. When it heard the noise of the falling pumpkin, it became terrified and ran away.

The foolish man saw the egg break in pieces. When he saw the rabbit running off he thought, "The baby horse has come out of its egg!" He jumped out of the pool and tried to catch the rabbit. He did not even have time to put on his clothes. He ran and ran, chasing it for a long time, but it is very hard work to catch a rabbit. And it was soon lost from his sight.

Feeling very sad about what had happened, he went back to his home and told his wife the whole story of the 'horse egg.' His wife was just as big a fool as he was. She said to him, "Why didn't you catch the colt and bring it here? I could have ridden him."

But hearing these words, the fool and his wife got into a big argument. The man shouted "If you ride on such a small horse, you'll break his back!" They fought so loudly that all the neighbors came to see what was the matter. The husband told them the story about the 'horse egg.' They all laughed because they had never heard of a horse laying eggs. They asked him to show them the broken egg. He took them to the pool where it had dropped, and they saw pieces of broken pumpkin.

Everybody started laughing again after seeing and hearing what had happened to this foolish couple.

The Nomads

any Tibetan nomads have never been to Lhasa, the capital of Tibet. Nomads considered a trip to Lhasa difficult, because they live an entirely different life style from the people in Lhasa.

Once, there were two neighbors who decided to go to Lhasa to sell Markong—butter, stuffed into raw hides and stitched into a large round ball about the size of a basketball. When the hide dries, it becomes airtight and prolongs the butter's freshness. They each had a load of butter and they set off on their journey to the cosmopolitan city of Lhasa.

After several days on foot, they finally arrived one evening. Since nomads always live in tents, that is what they expected to see. Instead, they saw two and three story stone houses.

As they stood around, completely dazed, not knowing what to do, a lady came by and asked if they were looking for a place to live. When they told her that they were, she decided to rent them the lower part of her house.

After moving into a house for the first time, they saw a staircase leading to the second floor. More surprisingly, their landlady had somehow got to the second floor without their noticing it.

While they were puzzling over this, a cat happened to come in and nimbly climbed upstairs with its four paws. One of them decided to emulate the cat and go upstairs. But the second one suggested that he should wait and see how the cat came down.

76

Before too long, the cat dashed downstairs on its four paws. They nodded and looked at each other with satisfaction at having learned this new way of climbing up and down the stairs.

One of them decided to go upstairs and speak with the landlady. He climbed up with his arms and legs without too much difficulty. But when he descended, emulating the cat—facing down, arms first and legs following, he came tumbling down the stairs.

His friend complimented him on his fast descent. Still laying flat on the floor, the other said, "It's fast if you don't mind landing on your face."

The next day, they decided to go downtown to sell their butter. As they were walking, they saw some pigs along the way. They had never seen pigs before and they appeared so peculiar to them. One asked the other, "What kinds of animals are those?"

He shrugged and said, "I don't know; what do you think they are?"

The first wondered and speculated, "I think they're either shrunken elephants or large rats."

The other said, "The way they grunt, they must be yaks. They're just hairless because of the warm climate here." They continued on.

Their path led them through a field where a farmer had left a hoe. Since nomads live entirely off animals, they have no idea of farming equipment. Out of curiosity, one of them stepped on the hoe, but handle flipped up and hit him hard on the knee. They thought the hoe was some sort of creature that kicks when disturbed, and they both ran away.

It was getting late, so they decided to return home. Their landlady had set up a kerosene lamp for them. Neither of them had ever seen a lamp like this. It gave off much more light than the oil-burning-wicks in their own village. They were so impressed by it, they wanted to buy one to take home.

The very next day, they went back to town to sell their butter and buy kerosene lamps. Since the word for 'lamp' is so different in their dialect, they decided to go to the shops and describe a lamp. They walked into a shop and asked, "Do you have the thing that you need at night, but not during the day?" The shopkeeper chased them out of shop thinking these two blockheads were insulting him.

They went to the next shop and described the lamp the same way. This shopkeeper also chased them out of his shop. Despite their humiliation, they were undaunted. At last one shopkeeper laughed and guided them to a whore house. He thought that is what they were looking for.

The two innocents walked in and asked, "Lady, we want something that's needed at night but not during the day. Do you have it to sell?"

The prostitute smiled and answered , "Yes, how much money do you have?"

"No money, but we'll swap you for butter," suggested the nomads.

She saw two loads of butterballs, and thought it would be a fine deal to take the butter for her services.

She led them to her bedroom and one by one she had intercourse with them. And she took all their butter. They had a good time with her, but now they had nothing to sell. They had to go back to their village empty handed.

In the village, their families were extremely disappointed that they had brought nothing in return for the butter. The first night each man went to his own wife. During intercourse, one of the men shouted to his wife, "Please talk to me like the lady in Lhasa! Kiss me like the lady in Lhasa! Work on me like the lady in Lhasa! I'll bring you the butter tomorrow."

Since nomad families all live in one large tent, there are no individual rooms for husband and wife. When the entire family heard his moaning pleas, they realized what he had done with the butter in Lhasa. They all jumped on him, beat him up and finally threw him out naked into the freezing cold. Not surprisingly, his partner was also there naked.

Kyakug "Dumbshit"

nce there was a tutor who taught out of his house. One of his pupils was not altogether too bright, so the other pupils nicknamed him 'Kyakug,' literally 'Dumbshit.'

The teacher not only gave lessons in reading and writing, but he also taught etiquette, the proper way to speak, and how to be a gentleman.

One day while Kyakug was studying with him, he saw the teacher's yaks returning from the hills. He shouted, "Teacher, Teacher! Your yaks are returning from the hills."

The teacher told him, "It's inappropriate to say 'your yaks,' because a teacher and pupil belong to one large family. Therefore, I want you to learn that a respectful pupil should say, 'Our yaks are returning from the hills.'"

Bearing this in mind, it became clear to Kyakug that everything around him must be addressed as "our."

One day, the teacher had some visitors. His wife was returning from fetching water. When Kyakug saw her, he quickly reported, "Teacher, Teacher! Our wife is coming home!" This left the guests wondering.

ⓖ

In Tibet most nuptials are arranged. The prospective groom goes around from family to family asking for their daughter's hand in marriage. Then the parents of the girls normally arrange some sort of interview with the young man.

Once there was a young man who was supposed to appear at the homes of three different families with marriageable daughters. This young man was not rich, so he borrowed a set of gold earrings to wear for the occasion to impress the families. He wore his best clothes and asked Kyakug to be his companion. Kyakug agreed and they set forth.

As is customary, the prospective groom's companion introduced the future groom to the family. Kyakug introduced his friend, "This is your future son-in-law. He's wearing all his nice clothes, but those earrings aren't his."

This turned the family off and they refused to give their daughter to such a show-off.

As they were on their way to the second family, the young man asked Kyakug, "Why did you have to say that these were not my earrings?" Kyakug promised not to tell anyone else.

They came to the second family. Again, Kyakug introduced the young man who wished to marry their daughter. Kyakug followed up his introduction by saying, "Oh, by the way, those are his own earrings."

This sounded so weird that the second family also refused to give their daughter.

As they proceeded to the third family, the young man scolded Kyakug. "Why do you keep bringing up my earrings? Just say nothing about them, my friend!"

They came to the third family and again Kyakug introduced the young man who wish to be their son-in-law. Finally he said, "Don't ask me about his earrings! I don't know anything about them."

The third family also refused to give their daughter in marriage.

❧

Kyakug was from a small village. He had never been to Lhasa, the capital of Tibet. Lhasa, where the Potala, the Dalai Lama's famous palace, is located, is the only cosmopolitan city in the country.

One day, Kyakug decided to go to Lhasa to sell Jiwa, dried yak dung, the main source of fuel. He had seven donkeys. He loaded the sacks of Jiwa on six of them and rode the other. When he arrived in Lhasa, he was completely overwhelmed by the sight of the Potala, the enormous immaculately white palace with thousands of windows built on a hill.

While goading his caravan of six donkeys, he started to count the windows of the palace out of total fascination. Since there were so many windows, it took him long time to count them.

All of a sudden, he remembered that he must count his own donkeys to make sure none was missing.

He counted only six donkeys, but he had started with seven. He counted again and again, but still came up with only six donkeys.

A feeling of panic surged through him. Thinking he had lost one of his donkeys, he ran around the open field looking for it. On the far side of the field he saw some tents where people were having a picnic.

Kyakug was in such an hysterical state, he even forgot the word for donkey. He hastily grabbed a handful of grass in one hand and picked up some donkey dung in the other. He dashed into one of the tents where people were having their picnic. By now he had even forgotten the word for tent. He ran into the tent and shouted, "Hey! You people in the sack! Have you seen my animal that eats this," showing them the handful of grass, "and shits this?" He showed them the donkey's dung.

Everyone in the tent burst into laughter at this stupid man's question.

Subdued by their laughter and his shame, he returned to his caravan and found all seven donkeys safely grazing. He had simply forgotten to count the one he was riding.

Rinjing Dorje, "Tibetan Storyteller," with his son, Guru, and daughter, Dewa, at his home in Seattle. Rinjing happily is encouraging his children to carry on his lineage of the Tibetan tradition of oral storytelling.

About the Author and Illustrator

RINJING DORJE is the son of Sherab Dorje from Kham, eastern Tibet, and Choe Gyalmo, a nomad lady from the foothills of the Himalayas. Sherab Dorje was recognized as the reincarnation of a Sherpa lama, Khamsum Wangdu, and in the 1930s he moved from his native land to northern Nepal.

Sherab Dorje was a highly esteemed practitioner of Tibetan medicine in healing the mentally ill. His uniquely unconventional techniques made him prominent throughout the region. Although the practice itself was a traditional Tibetan one, he formulated his own method, which called for keeping the patient in total darkness providing only light from a flickering butter lamp. He would then walk on the patient while reciting incantations and burning an intoxicating incense of Gugul, a powerfully scented sap. Then, he would glance commandingly into the eyes of his patient, while giving him counsel. Finally, he would prescribe some mineral and herbal medications. As a reward for curing a princess of Nepal's royal Rana family, he was made governor of an area in northern Nepal.

In the course of his official duties, he travelled extensively throughout that region. He met a beautiful young nomad lady, Choe Gyalmo, in the village of Shabru, and they were soon married. She gave birth to Rinjing Dorje 1949, the Tibetan year of the Earth-Ox.

As a young boy, Rinjing Dorje tended his family's live stock, herding their yaks, dris, sheep and cows on the high pastures of the Himalayas. It was then, sitting around the crackling camp fires, that Rinjing heard the amusing tales of the ever-popular Uncle Tompa from the other herders.

At the age of eleven, young Rinjing fell ill with some unknown malady. His father was unable to cure him. As a last resort, his parents consulted a renowned astrologer who advised Rinjing to become a monk. "Only then will he enjoy his full life," was the celestial computation.

Rinjing Dorje took the vows of a novice monk and joined Muen Monastery in Tibet. When Rinjing was thirteen, his father suddenly passed away. He and his mother moved to Kathmandu where his father had built a monastery.

There Rinjing attended Western-style schools and came into contact with Westerners. Later, in the hopes of becoming a writer, he went abroad to further his education.

To date, he has published two books in English. He is currently completing the manuscript of his first novel. He and his two children live in the Seattle area, where he is also a noted storyteller of Tibetan tales.

ADDISON SMITH, an American by birth, has been living for the past two decades in the mountains of Nepal. His artistic and creative existence can best be compared to that of Tibetan mountain nomad. He beautifully shares that experience through his illustrations.